LEGENDARY LIVES

Anne Frank

by Kate Moening
Illustrated by Claudia Marianno

 BELLWETHER MEDIA
MINNEAPOLIS, MN

Blastoff! Missions takes you on a learning adventure! Colorful illustrations and exciting narratives highlight cool facts about our world and beyond. Read the mission goals and follow the narrative to gain knowledge, build reading skills, and have fun!

Traditional Nonfiction

Narrative Nonfiction

Blastoff! Universe

MISSION GOALS

> FIND YOUR SIGHT WORDS IN THE BOOK.

> LEARN ABOUT ANNE FRANK'S LIFE.

> LEARN ABOUT HOW ANNE FRANK'S DIARY INSPIRES PEOPLE.

This edition first published in 2026 by Bellwether Media, Inc.

No part of this publication may be reproduced in whole or in part without written permission of the publisher. For information regarding permission, write to Bellwether Media, Inc., Attention: Permissions Department, 3500 American Blvd W, Suite 150, Bloomington, MN 55431.

Library of Congress Cataloging-in-Publication Data

LC record for Anne Frank available at: https://lccn.loc.gov/2025018599

Text copyright © 2026 by Bellwether Media, Inc. BLASTOFF! MISSIONS and associated logos are trademarks and/or registered trademarks of Bellwether Media, Inc. Bellwether Media is a division of FlutterBee Education Group.

Editor: Rebecca Sabelko   Designer: Andrea Schneider

Printed in the United States of America, North Mankato, MN.

This is **Blastoff Jimmy**! He is here to help you on your mission and share fun facts along the way!

Table of Contents

Meet Anne Frank	4
A New Life	6
Anne's Diary	10
The Diary Lives On	18
Glossary	22
To Learn More	23
Beyond the Mission	24
Index	24

Anne Frank writes in her **diary**. She writes about what she thinks and sees. She dreams of being an **author** one day.

A New Life

It is 1933. The **Nazis** have taken over Germany. They have made it unsafe for **Jewish** people.

Anne's Diary

It is Anne's 13th birthday! Her parents give her a diary.

Anne is excited to start writing. She writes about her friends and her birthday party.

The Nazis want to send Anne's sister away. But Anne's family hides in a secret attic.

Four other Jewish people hide with them. Their friends sneak in food.

▶ JIMMY SAYS ◀

Anne's father owned a business. The secret attic was above the business.

Anne writes in her diary often. She writes about her fears and dreams.

radio

Anne hears the **Dutch minister** on the radio. He asks people to save their war diaries. He says the diaries are part of history.

The Diary Lives On

JIMMY SAYS
The secret attic is now a museum. It is called the Anne Frank House.

Anne's father published her diary. Anne's dream came true.

People all over the world read Anne's diary. Her words **inspire** people to have hope during hard times.

Anne Frank Profile

Born
June 12, 1929, in Frankfurt, Germany

Died
February or March 1945

Accomplishments
Writer who kept a diary of her experiences as a Jewish girl in hiding during World War II

Timeline

1934: Anne moves to the Netherlands to escape Nazi Germany

1942: Anne and her family go into hiding in a secret attic above her father's business

1942 to 1944: Anne writes about life and her experiences in hiding

1944: The Nazis find the secret attic and imprison Anne and her family

1947: Anne's father, Otto, has her diary published so that the world will know her story

Glossary

author–a person who has written something

diary–a book where someone writes down their personal thoughts, feelings, and experiences

Dutch minister–the leader of the Netherlands

inspire–to give someone an idea about what to do or create

Jewish–related to Judaism, a religion that began in Israel and teaches belief in one God

Nazis–members of the party that controlled Germany from 1933 to 1945; Adolf Hitler led the Nazis.

publish–to print for a public audience

World War II–the war from 1939 to 1945 that involved many countries

To Learn More

AT THE LIBRARY

Harding, Thomas. *The House on the Canal: The Story of the House That Hid Anne Frank.* Somerville, Mass.: Candlewick Studio, 2025.

Lowell, Barbara. *Behind the Bookcase: Miep Gies, Anne Frank, and the Hiding Place.* Minneapolis, Minn.: Kar-Ben Publishing, 2020.

Pincus, Meeg. *Anne Frank.* Ann Arbor, Mich.: Cherry Lake Publishing, 2025.

ON THE WEB

FACTSURFER

Factsurfer.com gives you a safe, fun way to find more information.

1. Go to www.factsurfer.com.

2. Enter "Anne Frank" into the search box and click 🔍.

3. Select your book cover to see a list of related content.

23

BEYOND THE MISSION

> WHAT FACT FROM THE BOOK DO YOU THINK WAS THE MOST INTERESTING?

> DO YOU WRITE IN A JOURNAL? WHAT DO YOU WRITE ABOUT?

> IF YOU WERE TO MEET ANNE FRANK, WHAT QUESTIONS WOULD YOU ASK HER?

Index

Anne Frank House, 20
attic, 12, 19, 20
author, 5
camp, 19
diary, 4, 5, 10, 15, 16, 17, 19, 20
dreams, 5, 15, 20
Dutch minister, 16
family, 7, 10, 12, 19, 20
food, 12, 19
friends, 10, 12, 19
Germany, 6, 8
hide, 12

Jewish, 6, 7, 9, 12
Nazis, 6, 8, 9, 12, 19
Netherlands, 7, 8
profile, 21
publish, 17, 20
radio, 16
World War II, 8, 16, 19
writes, 5, 10, 15